Written by Tim Bugbird.
Illustrated by Nadine Wickenden.

God's love in my heart

Tim Bugbird • Nadine Wickenden

Big and Boo were resting
after bouncing in the forest all day.
They were a long way from home,
and Boo was very tired.

"I don't think I can make it all the way back to the burrow," said Boo. "My paws are just too sore!"

Big smiled and took Boo's hand.

"Well, I know you can," said Big.

"And do you know why?"

"Because God's love in our hearts makes us strong!"

As they walked, Big began to explain . . .

God's love is so sweet.
It can scent every flower.

God's **love**
is so **calm**.
It turns **storms**
into showers.

God's love
is so big.
It soars up
past the trees.

It's mighty enough

to rush streams

towards the seas.

God's love is so bright.

It can light up the night . . .

and **softly** cap mountains with **blankets** of **white.**

God's love
is so happy.
Grey skies turn to blues.
His love paints each rainbow
with colourful hues.

His love is so endless.

It goes on and on

and carpets your pathway,

no matter how long.

God's love is so big. It's amazing. It's huge!
Wait, can you feel it? It lives inside you!

With God's love
in our hearts, we can be really strong
and do kind and thoughtful things all the day long!

Before they knew it, Big and Boo were home, snuggled up in their cosy burrow.

"Isn't God's love amazing?" Big whispered to Boo.

But Boo was sound asleep, dreaming of God's big love.

THE END